201 Little
Buddhist Reminders

201 Little Buddhist Reminders

Gathas for Your Daily Life

Barbara Ann Kipfer

Ulysses Press

Published by:
ULYSSES PRESS
P.O. Box 3440
Berkeley, CA 94703
www.ulyssespress.com

ISBN 1-56975-518-3
Library of Congress Control Number 2005908368

Printed in Canada by Transcontinental Printing

2 4 6 8 6 10 9 7 5 3 1

Acquisitions Editor: Ashley Chase
Editorial/Production: Claire Chun, Lily Chou
Cover Photo: John Arbogast/Digital Vision/Getty Images
Cover Design: Robles-Aragón, Bryce Willett
Interior Design: Robles-Aragón, Leslie Henriques

Distributed by Publishers Group West

Table of Contents

▲ ▼ ▲

Introduction

▲ ▼ ▲

We are often overwhelmed, feeling busy so much of the time. We forget what we are doing and even who we are. We forget to look at the people we love and really appreciate them. Even when we have free time, we fill it with mindless activity like watching television or reading magazines. Very rarely do we stop doing things, be quiet, pay attention.

Gathas are short verses that you can recite during the day to help you attend to the present moment. In Buddhist literature, gatha is sometimes used to mean a verse from the sutras (Buddhist scripture), but it also refers to little poems that can be used to encourage mindfulness. Some gathas are found in Zen and some belong to Buddhism generally.

Unlike a mantra, which is the same for all occasions, we can have specific gathas for specific activities. I've designed the original gathas in this book to focus on the activities and concerns of modern everyday life. Gathas help you stop for a few moments and check in with your body, mind, action, and intention. In this way, you can weave a meditative rhythm and sensibility into your daily routine, no matter how busy it might be.

When you focus your mind on a gatha, you return to yourself and become more aware of what you are doing. When you are finished reciting a gatha, you can continue what you are doing with heightened awareness. For example, when you are listening to music, you can recite, "Listen, listen. These wonderful sounds bring me back to my true self." This is an example of being in the present moment, really being there in true appreciation.

Gathas focus on the small everyday things of life and express how all beings and things are interconnected. The gatha form can become a very meaningful way for you to reconnect, to feel an interconnectedness in any situation. We spend our lives individuating, separating—

making me, you, separate and distinct. Our minds are constantly writing the story of "my life" with me as the star and everyone else as supporting players. But this creates suffering for us, this desire to "be somebody" separate. Gathas help us be in the present moment, stop writing the story, and reconnect to life and other people.

Gathas may be said at any time or in any place, because you say them silently to yourself. It is a beautiful practice to acknowledge what you are doing and bring a sense of the sacred to your life instead of mindlessly experiencing things as one task or errand or routine action after another. Mundane activities like washing dishes and taking out the garbage can become opportunities to bring you back to the sacredness of the present moment.

There are gathas for waking in the morning, for eating a meal, for having tea or coffee, for appreciating nature, and many other occasions in everyday life. Gathas can also speak to issues in our lives—developing our mindfulness and concentration; dealing with sadness, fear, or depression; controlling our anger; eating and weight issues; establishing better relations with our partners, friends, children, or parents; being more focused at work, and so on.

A gatha is not a mantra to be memorized and repeated. A gatha should be held, like a precious baby, and cuddled. If used judiciously and mindfully, a gatha can offer you great energy and power. A gatha can heal and soothe. Most of all, they are reminders on the path. They are mini meditations.

To meditate is to become aware of what is going on in our minds, feelings, bodies, and environment. Settling into the present moment, we experience the beauty and wonder without seeking elsewhere. Meditation teaches us that being aware is being happy.

The mindfulness that we practice in meditation needs to be carried over to ordinary life. This is where it gives us its greatest rewards. Practicing mindfulness of the body, feelings, and mind when you do ordinary things like walk, drive, work, care for others, or do the most mundane things can be a new challenge. This is where gathas can help.

When we practice with gathas, we live in awareness. We have more calm, concentration, joy, and peace. We share these with others. The world becomes more calm, joyous, peaceful.

How to Use This Book

There are more than two hundred gathas in this book. Each gatha is devoted to something that is an integral part of everyday living. They have been organized into simple categories: relationships, work, health, spiritual path, and more. The first section (gathas for beginners) provides twelve gathas that are easy to incorporate into your daily routine right away.

When you read the title of any of the gathas in the book, take a few moments and ask yourself if the topic resonates with you, if it is associated with your life in a meaningful or timely way. When you land on one that touches you, use it as an aid to your spiritual practice. Read the gatha thoughtfully. Read it slowly.

If you have trouble concentrating on the gatha while reading it, please do try to memorize it. You might find it easier to remember if you copy it down a couple of times. If you have trouble remembering one, try to memorize only the key words from each line. That will be enough for you to gain the benefits of using a gatha.

As you go about your day, inwardly recite the gatha while you do the activity it accompanies. Try doing this as a mindfulness exercise, to focus your attention and bring you to the present moment. You can use conscious breathing (breath awareness) as part of this mindfulness practice. A line or phrase or clause can be matched to an in-breath or an out-breath. The first line, breathe in. The second, breathe out, etc. Each gatha sets a "direction" for mindfulness, and the breath grounds this.

You can also use gathas as part of a meditation practice. Meditation can take on many forms, but the most simple is just to set aside a time every day, a regular time and place. Set the amount of time, a reasonable amount of time for your lifestyle and personality. Eliminate distractions, wear comfortable attire, and sit on a cushion or in a chair. Then let your eyes close gently, focus on your breath, watch thoughts drift by, let them go, and come back to your breath. When you decide to add gathas, pick one or two of them and give them your whole attention as you meditate.

Working through all of the gathas over time will gradually make you more aware, more mindful. What were once mundane experiences become poetic. Things start to slow down and take on new meaning. You will be more present.

Please do also think about creating your own verses to match particular circumstances in your life. You can create these mini meditations and mini poems yourself. Composing new verses enriches the tradition. (See "A Note on Gathas" on page 244 for a format to follow if you like.) You can make up your own gatha for any activity you want to approach in an especially mindful way.

GATHAS FOR

beginners

GATHA FOR . . .

opening the curtains

▲ ▼ ▲

I open the curtains to a new day. I look upon this morning as a rebirth and understand that only this one day exists.

turning on the water

▲ ▼ ▲

As I turn on the water, my body's essence pours before me. Clouds, oceans, rivers, and deep wells all support my life.

GATHA FOR . . .

morning tea or coffee

This drink is my cup of mindfulness. I hold the present moment in my hands.

simple living

Our lives are often filled with a million things to do and consume that distract us from simple living. When I pay attention and become mindful, I marvel at the simple things in life that I once passed over. Consuming less and living simply are the true conditions for happiness.

a stop sign

When I see a red light or a stop sign, I smile at it and thank it. I see it as a friend, helping me to resist rushing. The sign says: Stop, Return to the Present Moment. May I meet the present moment with joy and peace. I breathe and smile.

answering the telephone

The telephone rings once, and I stay where I am and breathe. Breathing in, I calm myself. Breathing out, I smile. The phone rings again, and I breathe again. It rings a third time, and I slowly move toward it. I pick up the phone in mindfulness and smile.

GATHA FOR . . .

making a decision
▲ ▼ ▲

Decisions can stir up powerful feelings. My thoughts are just thoughts—they are not me or reality. Which choice will benefit others? Which choice will move me toward peace?

arriving home

I have arrived, I am home, in the here and now. I am solid, I am free. In the ultimate I dwell. My mind can go in a thousand directions. Now I walk in peace. Each step a warm breeze. With each step, a lotus blooms.

201 Little Buddhist Reminders

eating

I am aware of the miracle of food and the miracle that it finds its way to my table. I am aware of the miracle of the body, that I have a system for digesting food, absorbing nutrients, and eliminating what I can't use. I eat slowly, mindfully, with awareness.

finding your center

To practice centering the mind is to build a home for yourself. I unify my mind so it is free, stable, unbound, centered. I let go and reside at the center of the circle, in the midst of everything.

201 Little Buddhist Reminders

turning on a light

▲ ▼ ▲

Ancient trees, water, and wind join my hand to bring light to this moment.

going to sleep

Falling asleep at last I vow with all beings to enjoy the dark and the silence and rest in the vast unknown.

GATHAS FOR

relationships

making friends

▲ ▼ ▲

Making friends with myself, I will then be able to make friends with others. A good friend is the finest companion. I look my friend in the eyes. I listen. I ask questions. I listen more.

strengthening a friendship

Our friends are not always what we would like them to be. But when a friendship is good, it is worth strengthening. I thank any friend who believes in me. I strengthen friendship by being generous, loving, loyal, and tolerant with my friends.

helping someone who is down

I set an example by speaking and acting in a positive manner. I walk the positive path. I demonstrate how to let go and not get caught up in angry thoughts, passionate thoughts, worried thoughts, or depressed thoughts. I practice mindfulness, mindful breathing, and smiling.

hugging

I am so happy to hug my dear _____. I know s/he is real in my arms. I mindfully meet this person with the grace of an open heart and open arms.

GATHA FOR . . .

kissing

May I kiss this person as if for the first time. May I enjoy the kiss for itself—not as a promise of sex. I will always be honest and gentle when it comes to sex.

love

The more love I extend, the more love I have. But to generate love, I must love myself first. Only here and now can we truly love—the past is a memory, the future is a fantasy. To say I love someone is not enough; I also need to be tolerant and respectful.

being a better mate or partner

Demonstrating my dedication, giving assurance of my commitment, and offering love and faithfulness—I seek to become a better partner. I am my partner's best friend and biggest fan.

listening

I need great skill in listening. I choose to be open and accepting and mindful. I take time now to sit quietly and listen. I am committed to cultivating loving speech and deep listening in order to bring joy and happiness to and relieve the suffering of others.

dealing with others'
bad behavior

▲ ▼ ▲

People act out their suffering in bad behavior.
Seeing this, I choose not to react and get myself
stuck in something that does not concern me.
I have absolutely no control over others' behavior,
but I can control my own.

being a better parent

When my child comes to me, I make sure I am really there. I do not think about the past or worry about the future. Children are a meditation.

talking with a child

▲ ▼ ▲

Children are given to us for a short while—to treat
with care and respect. Children love respect—for
their needs and fears. I offer the greatest respect
by being fully present in the moment with children,
deeply listening. If I listen and speak mindfully,
the children will learn to do the same.

dealing with difficult parents

Being present and aware with my family is an amazing, liberating feeling. I bring generosity, mindfulness, and patience to this moment. These energies bring about the opening of my inner nature so I can rest in peace and promote unity.

dealing with neighbors

▲ ▼ ▲

I was born with innocence and purity, and so were my neighbors. What we are taught and what we learn alter us. But, underlying this, we all have Buddha-nature. May I fully appreciate every neighbor I encounter. Each brings beauty and Buddha-nature to this world.

a pet

▲ ▼ ▲

I love my pet unconditionally and with gratitude. With great care, I meet the pet's needs and expect nothing in return. I gratefully accept the companionship, loyalty, and unconditional love that my pet gives to me. We are interconnected and I cherish the relationship.

serving food

▲ ▼ ▲

Focusing my attention on the people who will share my meal, I stay in the present moment. I feel love and appreciation for this opportunity to both have food to serve and people to share it with. Loving intent is part of my serving.

selecting a gift

Thoughtfulness is the key when I choose a gift for someone. I know that the thought behind it is more important than how much I spend. I do not expect anything in return. I feel joy before giving this gift.

wrapping a gift

▲ ▼ ▲

I make gift wrapping a meditation. As I choose the paper, size it, fold it around the gift, and decorate the package with a bow or ribbon, I hold an image of the recipient in my mind. I meditate on the joy of giving my love and attention to that person.

giving someone a gift

I give this gift gracefully. When I present the gift, I also give the person the gift of my undivided attention.

GATHA FOR . . .

helping another
▲ ▼ ▲

I help others with no thought of personal gain.
I do not wish to be recognized for helping. I also
see that helping myself is the first condition for
helping others.

praying for another

May all beings be happy, content, and fulfilled. May all beings be healed and whole. May all have whatever they need. May all beings be protected from harm and freed from fear. May all enjoy inner peace and ease. May all be awakened, liberated, and free. May there be peace in this world and universe.

GATHAS FOR

work

turning on a computer

▲ ▼ ▲

I take three mindful breaths before turning on the computer. I greet it with a nod. I use the computer with calmness.

balancing work and personal life

Work is empty without a personal life, and a personal life is lacking without fulfilling work. They sometimes pull me in opposite directions, but each supports the other. Mindfulness, moderation, and patience help me balance these complementary aspects of life.

being a better employee

▲ ▼ ▲

The Buddha said great employees start work before the boss and stay after the boss. They strive to do the work well and uphold the employer's good name. I treasure bosses for the difficulty they bring—it's another opportunity for meditation in action.

preparing to start a work task

▲ ▼ ▲

Total absorption in the task is what I seek. I use skillful effort to create a focused mind, allowing clarity and concentration for completion of this task.

GATHA FOR . . .

dealing with annoying coworkers

▲ ▼ ▲

I choose to see the Buddha-nature even in people who are annoying. When I can no longer be annoyed by those who are annoying, I will find most everything agreeable.

organizing something

To be organized means I have set priorities, that I care deeply about the outcome. I reflect on what is truly of value, what gives meaning to life. I then set my priorities for organizing on that basis.

achieving a goal

In setting goals, I abandon useless states of mind. I concentrate my efforts and use self-discipline to achieve the goal. I do not waste energy on distractions.

dealing with conflict or difference of opinion

▲ ▼ ▲

Observing my opinions, I see them form and melt like snowflakes. I let go of my opinions, and of my concern for others' opinions. I choose not to argue with others, but rather think about ideas with them.

sitting down to write

▲ ▼ ▲

Writing is about listening to my inner voice, not just composing meaningful sentences. My writing becomes a meditation. I will write and release, without judging. I can edit later!

integrity

I choose to do my job and live my life with integrity, compassion, mindful observance, and a healthy sense of humor. In both large and small matters, may I always be true to my deepest principles so that my integrity may be a gift to others.

GATHA FOR . . .

managing time

▲ ▼ ▲

I choose not to waste time on desires and their
emptiness. I vow to overcome desire and when
I do this, I experience an increase in energy and
understanding—and, therefore, time.

finding money

I am already rich with life. Finding money is an
added blessing and I wish to be wise with it.

learning something new

▲ ▼ ▲

Ready to learn, I pose questions. I pause and give myself time to find an answer. Learning is a great source of happiness. To make a contribution to the world, I continue to learn.

correcting a mistake

The greatest mistake is to be continually fearful of making one. A stumble may prevent a fall. I admit I have made a mistake. My eyes are open wide to the consequences. This is an experience I learn from. That is the ultimate correction.

developing a mission

▲ ▼ ▲

My mission is not merely to work hard and carry out daily business. These are only the means of achieving the real mission, which is to better the welfare of the world.

staying focused

Focusing my effort on the present, I aim and sustain
my attention. I focus on one thing at a time and let
the imperfections of life be. Walking the path of
awakening is about progress, not perfection.

GATHA FOR . . .

problems at work

▲ ▼ ▲

When things fall apart on the job I vow with all beings to use this regretful energy and pick up the pieces with care.

discipline

I work to sustain effort and sincerity, discipline and self-control. I build from the practice of restraint, settling back and allowing desires to arise and pass without always feeling the need or compulsion to act on them. I work toward wisdom.

ethics

Through mindful attention and nonattachment, I
make my daily life sacred by practicing ethical
restraint, morality, and sincere virtue. I see how
comfortable, relaxed, free, and peaceful I feel
when I act ethically.

taking a test

I have done the best I can to prepare for this test.
Concentration is the essence of learning. Now, I will
concentrate on the questions and do the very best I
can to answer them. No matter what, I will continue
my learning.

managing money

I possess my money—it does not possess me.
Money can be helpful or harmful, can further either
good or evil, depending on whether I use it or abuse
it. I use my money wisely.

task completion

The past is gone and no one can predict the future. My task is here in the present moment. It is useless to worry or project, expending energy that I need to complete the task. I am here, NOW, focusing on this task. I smile to myself and say, completing this task is the most important job in my life.

turning off a computer

The computer is like a mind with thousands of interfaces. As I turn it off, I recognize its contribution to my life.

developing a path of service

I develop a generous heart, kind speech, and a life
of service and compassion. I, like everyone else,
want freedom from suffering. I actively serve others
to promote their welfare and relieve their suffering.

GATHAS FOR

everyday

waking up

▲ ▼ ▲

As I wake up, I welcome a new day, a mindful smile with each breath. May I live each moment with compassion and awareness.

troubling dreams

Regarding everything that occurs as if it is a dream, I simply disregard dreams that occur at night. I stay in the present moment, pay attention to direct experiences of sight and sound, smell and taste, bodily sensations. I awaken.

the first steps of the day

▲ ▼ ▲

As I take my first step, my foot kisses the floor. With gratitude to the earth, I walk in liberation.

dressing

I choose clothes that make me feel good. I do not need to impress anyone or tell people who I am through my style of dress. Instead I dress for the season or weather, dress tastefully and comfortably.

GATHA FOR . . .

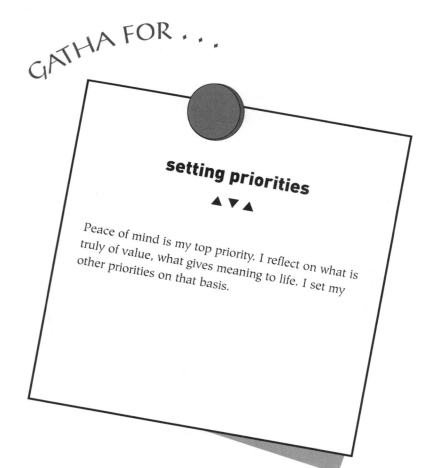

setting priorities

▲ ▼ ▲

Peace of mind is my top priority. I reflect on what is truly of value, what gives meaning to life. I set my other priorities on that basis.

preparing coffee or tea

▲ ▼ ▲

I train myself to drink my coffee or tea mindfully.
Doing only this, preparing and then drinking my
coffee or tea, I live the present moment.

reading a newspaper or magazine

I am aware that what I take in from media like newspapers and magazines affects my karma. I choose carefully. I do not fill my mind with harmful or disturbing information. When I am done with a newspaper or magazine, I share it with someone else who may appreciate it.

flushing the toilet

My body's waste is compost. Down the hopper it goes, returning to the earth.

GATHA FOR . . .

entering a room

▲ ▼ ▲

Entering this room, I see the present moment.
I bow to the room and breathe. I vow to enter
with calmness and awareness.

driving

This car is my legs. It goes where I choose. When I drive with awareness, everyone lives in safety.

GATHA FOR . . .

waiting

Waiting is the practice of patience. I develop my ability to wait and to listen, going deep into stillness. It is seeking without seeking. Deep slow breaths help me practice waiting in the present moment.

buying something

My happiness cannot be bought. What satisfies me is not the possession of the wanted object, but putting an end to the painfulness of desire. I remind myself of this when considering a purchase.

drinking water

▲ ▼ ▲

Water flows, it never fights. It is flexible, yet persistent enough to wear down rocks and carve out continents. I hear the sound of water gently falling into the glass as a soothing lullaby. Water helps bring my awareness to exactly where I am.

taking a nap

I am taking a nap because I feel a lack of vitality, fogginess, or sleepiness. I do not judge or suppress these feelings. I am mindful of and observe the feelings and take a nap with awareness. I wish to awaken with mindfulness.

preparing a meal

▲ ▼ ▲

Eating a meal in mindfulness is an important practice. I make the time I assemble a dish or meal into a meditation. I breathe in and out, getting in touch with the ingredients. In this food, I see clearly the presence of the entire universe that supports my existence.

after a meal

My plate is empty. My hunger is satisfied and my body's strength is fully restored. I use my power for the benefit of all. May all beings have the nourishment they need.

GATHA FOR . . .

bathing

▲ ▼ ▲

When I take a bath, I do so slowly and mindfully. I feel light and refreshed. Let this mindfulness carry on into the next activity I engage in.

reading a book

I choose my books carefully, knowing that some books can be toxins just as foods can be toxins. I read slowly and calmly so that the very act of reading is peace. During the time I read, I stop every half hour, close my eyes for a minute or so, and bring my attention back to my breath.

brushing your teeth

▲ ▼ ▲

Brushing my teeth, outside - inside - underneath, and rinsing, I take the vow to speak purely and lovingly. Cleaning is not enough. When my mouth offers only wisely chosen speech, I sow beautiful seeds in the garden of my heart and life.

GATHAS FOR

occasions

GATHA FOR . . .

a birthday

▲ ▼ ▲

Another celebration of being here. May I live all the present moments of my life. I begin at once to live and count each day as a separate life.

preparing a celebration

May I be fully present in preparing for this celebration, cultivating generosity, gratitude, and kindness. I also know that I must cultivate generosity, gratitude, and kindness for even the smallest joys and wonders. Conditional happiness dependent upon a specific circumstance always leads to suffering. This celebration is a source of happiness if I use it to practice being in the present moment.

political choices

▲ ▼ ▲

Politics are necessary as a tool to solve human problems. We have political choices to make and a chance to be involved in changing the world. I gather strength and think carefully before I decide. I hope to make choices that will change what needs changing.

being a responsible citizen

▲ ▼ ▲

Speaking and acting on only what is true and useful and speaking wisely and appropriately are ways to be a responsible citizen in a community. To be a good citizen, I can protect life, practice generosity, behave responsibly, and consume mindfully.

flying in an airplane

▲ ▼ ▲

Putting my faith in those who will carry me from one place to another, I look at the road as home. Reaching my destination, I am grateful.

vacationing

Going on vacation, I leave work at the workplace. I truly enjoy and am in the present moment of the vacation. When there are appropriate times, I meditate or set up mini-retreats.

returning from vacation

▲ ▼ ▲

Upon my return, I live as if I was on vacation—
savoring every minute and collecting memories.
Life is an extended working vacation.

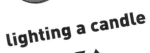

lighting a candle

Respectful of the power of fire, I calmly light this candle, brightening the room and lives that see that candle. I light the candle mindfully and therefore shine the light of awareness. The sole purpose of human existence is to kindle a light in the darkness of mere being.

drawing or painting

▲ ▼ ▲

To this artwork, I bring concentration, effort, and patience. I enter into this activity without judgment, simply being present and fully aware of what I am doing. I am grateful for the ability to create artwork.

appreciating art

▲ ▼ ▲

I mindfully acknowledge the expressions conveyed in this art. The art created by others is amazing, reflecting their inner life. I look around and feel joy in colors and shapes. I enjoy and appreciate what is before my eyes.

GATHA FOR . . .

listening to music

▲ ▼ ▲

Listening to music, I feel reverence. With mindfulness, I open my senses and open my heart to the emotions the music inspires. I hear all sounds as beautiful music; I hear music in all things.

watching television

▲ ▼ ▲

Mind and television receive what I choose. I select well-being and nourish joy.

GATHA FOR . . .

turning off the television

▲ ▼ ▲

The off button brings peace and quiet; it brings me
to myself. I turn off TV and turn on life!

going to a party

Even at a party, I speak and act wisely. I know that every action of body, speech, and mind has consequences, a corresponding result. Deep listening and moderation is my mantra in this situation.

GATHA FOR . . .

eating at a restaurant

▲ ▼ ▲

In choosing to eat at a restaurant, I recognize the many hands who have worked to provide me with nourishment. May I appreciate that work and the experience of eating food that has been prepared by those caring hands.

GATHAS FOR

housework

taking the garbage out

In the garbage, I see beauty. In beautiful things, I see the garbage. One cannot exist without the other. Everything changes, everything is impermanent. I meditate on the garbage, which teaches me about impermanence and the happiness in not grasping.

cleaning

As I clean this room, I make it fresh and calm and boundless joy and energy arise in me. My heart and mind grow clearer with this experience.

clearing out clutter

▲ ▼ ▲

I reduce undue clutter and complexity by giving away or selling possessions that are seldom used or could be used productively by others. Today I learn to touch the earth more gently, living with less complexity and clutter. The path is swept and I see the ground of awakening.

feeding an animal

In this dish of pet food, I clearly see the presence of the entire universe supporting the existence of this animal. I am grateful to have food to serve. This feeding is a show of love and respect. Animals teach us all about unconditional love and gratitude.

doing laundry

▲ ▼ ▲

As I sort clothes for a laundry load, I am mindful of the effort it took to make the clothes and the machines that will care for them. As I do my part, my mind is still. I rejoice in having fresh, clean clothes.

finding something that was misplaced

▲ ▼ ▲

Impermanence is revealed in the magical reappearance of something lost. I am not here forever. Every person and thing is making a guest appearance.

GATHA FOR . . .

preparing food

▲ ▼ ▲

Earth, water, sun, and air, all live in this food I prepare. I feel gratitude for my food and all those beings involved in bringing it to my table. I prepare the meal with love and compassion, knowing that these feelings will nourish those I am feeding.

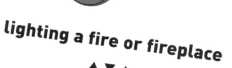

lighting a fire or fireplace

▲ ▼ ▲

Respectful of its power, I calmly light the fire. A wild fire destroys, but a controlled fire brightens and comforts. I appreciate fire—one of the four elements of the universe—for giving us warmth and fueling our cooking.

GATHA FOR . . .

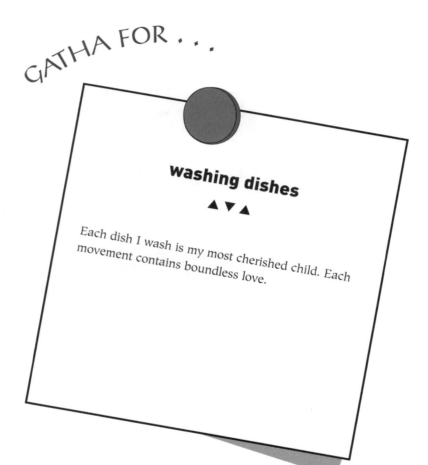

washing dishes

▲ ▼ ▲

Each dish I wash is my most cherished child. Each movement contains boundless love.

sweeping the floor

▲ ▼ ▲

As I carefully and mindfully sweep the floor, I experience understanding. If I am mindful of the path, it acts as the ground or floor of my awakening.

GATHAS FOR

talking

GATHA FOR . . .

wise speech

Speech should be wise, kind, and minimal. Before I speak I am mindful of what I am doing, how I am feeling, and what my motivation is. I talk only when necessary.

expressing an idea

There is no need to worry that a good idea or the solution to a problem will be lost; what is of value will be available at the proper moment. I open my mind and dance with ideas instead of fixating on them.

expressing an opinion

▲ ▼ ▲

Each comment I make is like a bubble that pops. I ask myself if I need to express this opinion or make this comment. More often than not, the answer is no. The comment is not beneficial, not timely, unnecessary.

quietness

Only a quiet and receptive mind can learn. I aim to learn a natural quietness of mind and openness of heart. The quieter I become, the more I can hear.

making a telephone call

▲ ▼ ▲

As I prepare to make a telephone call, may my words create mutual understanding and even love. May my words be thoughtful, skillful, and beneficial. I make the telephone call with awareness and mindfulness.

apologizing

Apologizing to someone I offended produces
marvelous and immediate relief for both of us.
I will apologize immediately as soon as I recognize
my thoughtlessness and lack of mindfulness.

forgiving

▲ ▼ ▲

Forgiveness is at the heart of all happiness. First I forgive myself. I acknowledge that everyone is still growing spiritually. I forgive past offenses. It is the way to heal and to appreciate the present moment.

giving advice

▲ ▼ ▲

When giving advice to others, I wish to have compassion and thoughts for their benefit. I offer advice only when asked.

keeping wise silence

It is beautiful and peaceful to stay in a place of silence of mind. I value silence and its eloquence.

praise or blame

I do not welcome praise or hide from blame. Neither praise nor blame moves the wise person.

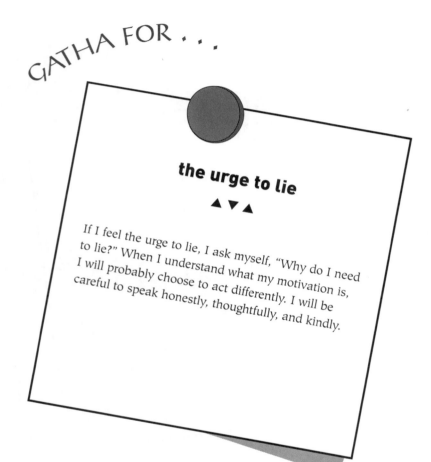

the urge to lie

▲ ▼ ▲

If I feel the urge to lie, I ask myself, "Why do I need to lie?" When I understand what my motivation is, I will probably choose to act differently. I will be careful to speak honestly, thoughtfully, and kindly.

dealing with arguments

Arguing is useless. To uproot the anger that starts an argument, I name it and give it space. I shine the light of awareness on it and it loses its power over me. I vow to be mindful of my speech.

GATHA FOR . . .

dealing with criticism

▲ ▼ ▲

A critic is a blessing. I look upon a person who is criticizing me as giving me a hidden treasure, as a wise person who shows me the dangers of life. Instead of defending myself, I accept the criticism (whether it is justified or not), study it, then let it go.

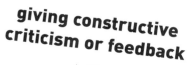

giving constructive criticism or feedback

▲ ▼ ▲

Each day, I intend to be generous, offer compliments, give accurate feedback, listen carefully.

humor

I choose to have a healthy sense of humor. I use gentleness and a sense of humor to settle down and stay present. I ask: will I even remember this situation in a few days, months, years?

teaching

The whole world is my teacher. What am I teaching others? I sit in stillness and listen. With a quiet mind, I find a way to teach kindness.

GATHAS FOR

health

GATHA FOR . . .

appreciating the body

▲ ▼ ▲

Intention allows synapses to connect and many hundreds and thousands of movements are carried out by my body each day. I appreciate the beauty of this system and what it allows me to do and experience.

choosing healthful food

The nourishment that comes from being kind to myself and others is the kind of food that stays with me. Each day, I move toward a diet of natural, healthy, simple food—away from highly processed foods, meat, and sugar.

beginning an exercise routine

▲ ▼ ▲

I enter this exercise with awareness. Such exercise joins mind and body. To strengthen my mind, I must strengthen my muscles. Exercise is a blessing for the whole day.

dealing with aging

Instead of trying to ward off aging, I welcome it. I am not defined by my age any more than any other characteristic, for I have no solid self. Rather, I appreciate the internal treasures I accumulate as each year goes by.

getting sick

▲ ▼ ▲

I shall not be angry with getting sick. Illness is
inescapable and I can choose to be at ease with and
even gain strength from illness. I free myself from
fear and am grateful for the blessing that the illness
will eventually go away. Everything is impermanent,
even sickness.

healing

▲ ▼ ▲

I must stop, calm down, and rest to heal. I cultivate receptivity and acceptance. I work to create the right conditions for healing by acknowledging my suffering, exploring it, then letting go.

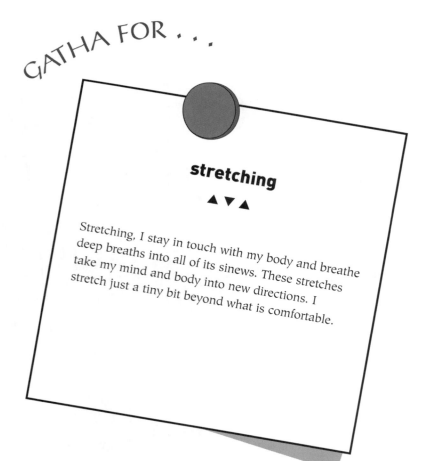

GATHA FOR . . .

stretching

▲ ▼ ▲

Stretching, I stay in touch with my body and breathe deep breaths into all of its sinews. These stretches take my mind and body into new directions. I stretch just a tiny bit beyond what is comfortable.

dealing with pain

Relaxing around the sensation of pain, I let pain be where it is. I discover that pain is inevitable but suffering is optional. I return to myself, practice mindful breathing, looking at these feelings, and smile. Doing this, I overcome pain.

going to a doctor or dentist
▲ ▼ ▲

Faith means trusting the unfolding process of life.
I let go of fears and attachments and open to the
unknown in this moment. My medical visit is a time
to practice my faith.

when you feel ill

Instead of pushing illness away, I hold it as I would hold a baby. I embrace it because suffering is part of life. I regard food and water and meditation and visualization of being well as medicine.

caring for a sick person

▲ ▼ ▲

I shall not forget that illness is part of our human existence. I shall not be angry with having to care for a sick person. Taking care of another, I help them become free from fear and grateful for the blessing that the illness will eventually go away.

dealing with overeating

There is no lasting peace through an attachment to a food. I ask myself, will a pint of ice cream bring happiness? If I overindulge, I create karma that will set me up to do it again. I choose to let go of this attachment.

dealing with death
and fear of death

▲ ▼ ▲

Keeping death at my fingertips puts my desires of
the moment into perspective. Unclouded by desires
and fantasies, I'm more open to love and generosity.
Death is not feared by one who has lived wisely.

saying no to drinking or drugs

▲ ▼ ▲

I am determined not to use alcohol or any other
intoxicant. These poisons damage my body and my
consciousness. Using them is a betrayal of myself
and the people around me. I will take in only
what helps me transform violence, fear, anger, and
confusion into mindfulness and peace in myself
and in society.

competing in sports or recreation

▲ ▼ ▲

Accepting and welcoming the chance to play and participate in sport or recreation, I remind myself that because I am not a competitor, no one in the world can compete with me.

GATHAS FOR

nature

GATHA FOR . . .

sunrise

▲ ▼ ▲

My path is lovely and deep, like the sunrise. I have a chance to see the sunrise and the dharma— to study it and practice with it. With the sunrise, I enter the world of great understanding.

gardening

The earth brings us life and nourishes us, then swallows up nutrients and starts all over. As I work in the yard and the garden, I see the birth and death in the earth's processes. I breathe and work with the earth. I prune the garden of my mind.

living on our planet

▲ ▼ ▲

I embrace a natural way of living, at least for one day, and I give the planet a much needed rest from my constant demands.

a flower

Earth and sky joined to create this flower. Its beauty is a gift. When I see a flower, I look deeply into the present moment and smile.

a budding tree

▲ ▼ ▲

Trees awaken with new buds in the spring and summer. Trees do not think; they just do their work. I rest like a great tree. I have to learn to become solid and stable like a tree, and be flexible, even in a storm.

the atmosphere

I am breathing all the time. Animals, plants, humans—we all breathe together. The atmosphere sustains me. I sustain the atmosphere by doing what I can to keep my air clean.

a rainstorm

The rain replenishes and sustains, but it can feel inconvenient and even uncomfortable. Without deciding rain is good or bad, I relax with the rain and feel whatever I am feeling. I choose to rain kindness on all.

201 Little Buddhist Reminders

looking out at the ocean

Living Zen means opening myself to a full awareness. I can use the storms, winds, and waves to
propel me through life. I must lose myself and
become one with the boat, water, and wind.

endangered species

▲ ▼ ▲

We are not separate from plants and animals. I defend all of them as I would my own life. I am part of the interconnected biosphere. I do what I can to protect an endangered species as I would care for a person who was ill.

metamorphosis
and seasonal change

▲ ▼ ▲

Everything changes. Everything evolves. Change is often different than we imagine, and it can make us feel angry or defeated if we let it. If I let go of everything and accept change, it is joyful. My mind remains centered and unmoved in the midst of change.

harmony

To live in harmony with the world, I exercise, sleep, and eat food that's healthy for my body and the planet. I aim to discover freedom and my own true nature. I walk in stillness, act in harmony.

the environment

I see what happens when waste is dumped and pollution poured into the air. Everything is interdependent. I choose to care for the world in the present moment and look out for its future.

a picnic

As I unwrap this picnic, I rejoice in the outdoors and in the food that will nourish us. I wish a happy picnic for all. Breathing in, we feel friendship and understanding. Breathing out, we smile.

a tree losing its leaves

Falling leaves remind me nothing is permanent.
When I watch the leaves falling and blowing
away, I feel joy. The changes of life are just as
they should be.

looking out a window

▲ ▼ ▲

It looks like the window separates me from things outside, but I am actually connected with the window and what is on the other side. We are not separate, but one. Looking with awareness, I see the oneness of all things.

watching a stream

▲ ▼ ▲

Letting go at the end of the out breath, letting the thoughts go, is like moving a boulder away so that water can keep flowing. I work toward having the patience to wait until the mind settles and the water is clear.

seeing clearly

▲ ▼ ▲

The way out of suffering is through seeing clearly.
Seeing the content of mind opens a path to freedom.
Seeing how everything arises and passing away, I
lessen grasping and greed. I see things as they are
instead of how I prefer them to be.

clearing snow

▲ ▼ ▲

Thousands of snowflakes have piled up. Mindfully, I gather them onto the shovel and place them aside, clearing a path. My path is mindfulness. On this beautiful path, I walk in peace.

the universe

▲ ▼ ▲

May all beings be happy, content, and fulfilled. May all beings be healed and whole. May all have whatever they need. May all beings be protected from harm and freed from fear. May all enjoy inner peace and ease. May all be awakened, liberated, and free. May there be peace in this world and universe.

sunset

As the sun sets, I practice the way of awareness. I vow to share the fruits of my life with all beings. I appreciate the numerous beings who gave guidance and support along my path today.

GATHAS FOR
feelings

happiness

▲ ▼ ▲

To achieve happiness, I must see that the one important time is now. The present moment is all I have. The happiness I seek will come from deep kindness and respect for all beings and all life. I am aware of what is appropriate, skillful, timely, and true.

bad times

I try to see difficult circumstances as bad-tasting medicine or learning experiences. I look at the reality of the situation without resistance, struggle, aversion, or avoidance. Everything is grist for the mill of awareness.

GATHA FOR . . .

moderation

Resolving to practice moderation, I gently learn to let go of extremes. Moderation is the only way to find true balance and the best way to live fully and with mindful awareness.

201 Little Buddhist Reminders

anger

Anger ruins joy, steals the goodness of my mind, and forces my mouth to say terrible things. Overcoming anger brings peace of mind, leads to a mind without regrets. If I overcome anger, I will be delightful and loved by all.

GATHA FOR . . .

compassion

▲ ▼ ▲

Seeing the web of suffering we become entangled in, I become kind and compassionate to others. This compassion includes myself. I start in this present moment to practice lovingkindness and compassion.

frustration

Instead of being frustrated, I must accept such instances either with humor, calmness, or constructive efforts to improve the situation. And when awareness is present, it displaces the kind of grasping that breeds frustration.

generosity

Knowing the power of a generous heart, I offer compliments, give accurate feedback, listen carefully. I cannot lose by being generous. If I have a greedy thought, I can replace it with a generous one. Every day is filled with opportunities to be generous.

laziness or procrastination

▲ ▼ ▲

I abandon sleepiness, dullness, and laziness and always exert enthusiastic effort.

201 Little Buddhist Reminders

alienation from others

▲ ▼ ▲

I see I am uncomfortable, rigid, grasping. I get upset or angry when someone disagrees with me or blames me for something, when things disappoint me or do not go my way, and even when somebody offers me constructive criticism. But I am not separate. I see that I am connected to all others, to everything. Now I feel relaxed and comfortable.

guilt

▲ ▼ ▲

Faced with guilt, I see that this emotion means I am not being aware. Allowing guilt feeds anxiety and fuels compulsive behavior. I choose awareness and motivate myself to learn and change so I may act more responsibly.

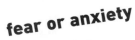

fear or anxiety

▲ ▼ ▲

Seeing fear and anxiety, I acknowledge it, see it as more stuff. Letting go of fear and anxiety, I feel calm arising. Happiness and love come naturally in letting go of fear and anxiety.

201 Little Buddhist Reminders

equanimity

The combination of effort, inner detachment, and genuine equanimity helps us come home within ourselves—and find inner peace. With equanimity, I can care for all beings without trying to control them. With equanimity, I react to unpleasantness with calm.

dislike and avoidance

▲ ▼ ▲

I recognize and acknowledge dislike and avoidance when it occurs. I stop feeding its fire. I try to stay with the direct experience. I work toward receiving each experience without judgment, grasping, dislike, or avoidance.

doubt

The remedy for doubt is more understanding. I recognize and see the doubt, then let it go. Letting go of doubt is a gift to myself.

GATHA FOR . . .

expectation

▲ ▼ ▲

My goal is to develop a mind which clings to nothing. If there is no clinging, no condemning, no expectations of how things should be—my mind will stay clear and balanced.

envy or jealousy

I see the ugliness of my envy and jealousy. Envy and jealousy stem from my inability to rejoice at someone else's happiness or success. I choose not to water these bad seeds.

good times

I appreciate good times. It is easy at this time to respond, not react. Whatever I cultivate during these good times gives me strength when things change. Difficulties arise in both good and bad situations and I am ready to respond wisely in both.

uncomfortable situations

In every situation where I feel discomfort, it is because I want something to be different. I am grasping after an idea I have about the way reality should be, rather than simply being present for what is. Dealing with discomfort is not passive acceptance but being aware of what really is in this moment.

greed or desire

▲ ▼ ▲

Feeling greedy, I think about the seed of the desire within me and the object of my desire. The point is not to kill desire; the point is to see it. Once observed, desire can no longer reign as the invisible commander of my actions. I gain more freedom.

restraint

Practicing conscious restraint with small desires gives me strength of mind when there are powerful desires. Restraint is seeing that wise activities bring greater happiness and understanding—and that unwise activities lead to further suffering and conflict.

GATHA FOR . . .

prejudice

Prejudice is a way of pushing the world away and sows bad seeds of karma. We all need less greed, less fear, less hatred, less prejudice. Without our personal prejudice and attachments, we develop a natural friendliness and contentment toward all our experiences and for all beings.

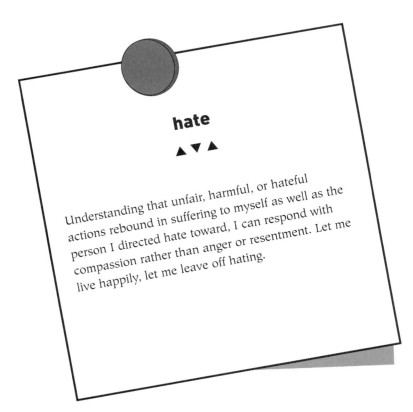

hate

▲ ▼ ▲

Understanding that unfair, harmful, or hateful actions rebound in suffering to myself as well as the person I directed hate toward, I can respond with compassion rather than anger or resentment. Let me live happily, let me leave off hating.

GATHA FOR . . .

irritation

▲ ▼ ▲

Instead of being angry over nuisances, irritations, and frustrations—I will accept such instances with either humor, serenity, or constructive efforts to improve the situation.

patience

True patience manifests itself as a non-grasping openness to whatever comes next. It is a calm willingness to be present. The true practice is patience, not wanting anything special or unusual to happen. The things I am attached to give me the opportunity to develop patience and kindness toward them and my grasping melts away.

dealing with restlessness

▲ ▼ ▲

Wondering how to get rid of restlessness, I acknowledge the state of mind, name it, and give it space. By shining the light of awareness on it, I break the power of restlessness over me.

reacting to things out of habit

▲ ▼ ▲

I recognize that I have many wants. I form habitual responses to things I dislike or seek to avoid. I may feel frustration or resistance to change. I choose a new thoughtful response instead of habitual responses I have resorted to in the past.

GATHA FOR . . .

working out a solution to a problem

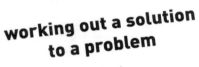

I seek to be grounded in calmness and moment-to-moment awareness. With awareness, I feel creative and see new options, new solutions to problems, and am able to maintain my balance and perspective in trying circumstances.

apathy and unconcern

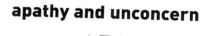

Rather than be indifferent or apathetic towards those people I do not know, I choose to open my heart and see the connectedness of all beings. I am not separate from them. With love and kindness, I open my heart and embrace others and the suffering of others. I wish an end of suffering for all beings.

feeling tired or burnt-out

▲ ▼ ▲

When I feel tired, what I really feel is resistance to tiredness. Tiredness is the product of a day filled with wasted thought, anxiety and worry, anger and resentment. These negative feelings sap my energy. When I let go of the resistance—I can watch the feeling of tiredness dissipate.

life's basic suffering

Suffering is what I feel when I want to be in a state other than what I am in—wishing I was elsewhere. Suffering is what happens when I struggle with whatever my life experience is. Instead, I take the antidote: resisting less, grasping less, and identifying with things less.

GATHAS FOR
the spiritual path

GATHA FOR . . .

morning meditation

▲ ▼ ▲

I meditate before I get out of bed by being grateful
for the opportunity to experience another day. I
thank the universe for the night of safety that passed
and for having a warm, dry place to sleep. Taking
three conscious breaths, I focus on the breath
entering and leaving my body.

mindfulness

▲ ▼ ▲

Mindfulness is loving all the details of my life. Right now, I come back to my breath with mindfulness.

faith

Faith means trusting the unfolding process of our lives—a willingness to let go of fears and attachments and open ourselves to the unknown in each new moment. I cultivate my faith, knowing it determines my destiny and is part of spiritual awakening.

stillness

Stop! I am just breathing. I calm the mind, let go of
the chatter, and allow a stillness to fall. In moments
of stillness and contentment, I notice the inner
workings of karma—cause and effect.

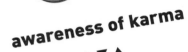

awareness of karma

▲ ▼ ▲

Each moment creates karma. I make opportunities with good and wise choices. My karma is made by thought, speech, and actions. If an ugly or unhelpful thought arises, I take care that it does not turn into speech or action.

breathing meditation

Each thought, each feeling creates the world. I hold joy and suffering tenderly in each breath.

calming the mind

Chasing after the world brings chaos. Allowing it all to come to me brings peace.

developing useful effort

I am alive in the present moment. Focusing my effort on the present, I experience a spaciousness and ease of mind which comes from letting go of attachments. The combination of useful effort and detachment from desires helps me find inner peace.

kindness

▲ ▼ ▲

The Dalai Lama says the main goal is to be kind. I stop before each action or word and weigh its kindness. I pay attention and give lovingkindness to my speech and my actions.

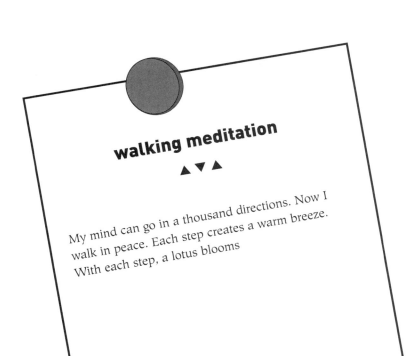

walking meditation

▲ ▼ ▲

My mind can go in a thousand directions. Now I
walk in peace. Each step creates a warm breeze.
With each step, a lotus blooms

GATHA FOR . . .

concentration

Zen is concentration on everyday routine. When I do something, I concentrate wholly on what I am doing. I put myself in a cocoon of concentration.

selflessness

If I have no-mind, then all my thinking and feeling
will not get between me and what I have to do. If I
have no-mind, I lose my ego. I become my doing.
May I break down the separation my mind makes
between Self and other so I may let go of ego and
see my interconnection to all beings.

GATHA FOR . . .

awareness

▲ ▼ ▲

I know I am breathing in. I know I am breathing out. I am aware of the hair on top of my head. I smile to the hair on my head. I am aware of the soles of my feet. I smile to the soles of my feet. I dwell in the present moment. I am aware this is the only moment when I am alive.

midday meditation

I use the midday mark as a mindfulness bell. I appreciate the half of the day that has passed and remind myself to be present in each moment of the rest of the day. I am aware of the blessings that surround me.

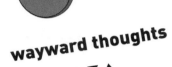

wayward thoughts

▲ ▼ ▲

To keep wayward thoughts from growing into evil intentions, I observe my thoughts constantly. Observation of thoughts is essential to my practice.

peace

When my actions are motivated by generosity, kindness, love, or wisdom, the results are happiness and peace. May I cultivate a silence of mind that brings this happiness and peace.

wisdom

I need more wisdom, not knowledge, and that comes from awareness. Wise activities bring happiness and understanding; unwise activities lead to suffering and conflict. I use restraint and gain strength and composure of mind to pursue a wise course.

motivation

I aim to make every action serve the goal of helping others. Even eating can have this motivation: I eat to maintain strength, prolong my life, and be better able to help others. I am always mindful of my motivations.

GATHA FOR . . .

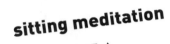

sitting meditation

▲ ▼ ▲

Sitting in the present moment, I breathe mindfully.
Each in-breath nourishes love; each out-breath,
compassion.

dealing with distractions

The mind is like a puppy, wandering endlessly and delighting in each new distraction. With amusement and great affection, I patiently gather my mind again and again as gently and lovingly as I would a puppy. By training my own mind, I cultivate the patience and equanimity to deal with other distractions.

GATHA FOR . . .

wartime

▲ ▼ ▲

I look deeply into the nature of war and I use it as an opportunity to be more aware. I use this practice to remind myself that violence always leads to more violence, anger to more anger. I use this practice to cultivate kindness, which leads to more kindness, and love, which leads to more love.

truth

Instead of creating ideas to hold on to, I can let go and open to the actual truth of each changing moment. I can find the truth right where I am. The world spins without my help, people do what they do, and my life will run its course one way or the other. Sometimes my plans do not work out. I can decide not to get upset about things over which I have no power.

insight meditation

▲ ▼ ▲

Every moment can be used to gain insight and
from that calm arises. I aim to practice constant
mindfulness. This brings tranquility and insight.
I can sustain wisdom even in the midst of ordinary
activities and distractions.

awareness of impermanence

▲ ▼ ▲

With precision, I watch the wave of impermanence. The temporariness of everything teaches me the principle of harmony. When I do not struggle against it, I am in harmony with reality.

observing my intentions

▲ ▼ ▲

I am mindful of my intentions. I take responsibility for my intentions and try to change any unskillful or harmful ones before they become actions or words. When I am in the present moment, I can be aware of my intentions, take responsibility for them, and have the possibility of transforming my actions and words to be only skillful and beneficial.

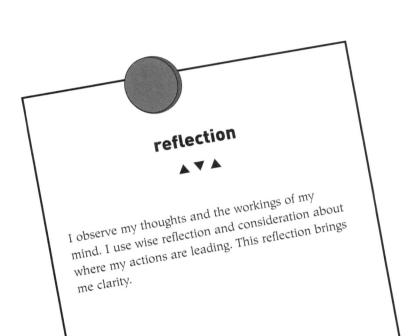

reflection

▲ ▼ ▲

I observe my thoughts and the workings of my mind. I use wise reflection and consideration about where my actions are leading. This reflection brings me clarity.

GATHA FOR . . .

integrating practice into daily activity

I am developing an integrated awareness of all the dimensions of my being. I make my body, my actions, my feelings and my relationships, my work and my play, all part of ongoing meditation.

evening meditation

I remind myself that life and death are important. Time passes swiftly by and opportunity is lost. I strive to awaken. I take heed. I do not squander my life.

learning

▲ ▼ ▲

My parents were my first teachers. In my formal education, instructors taught me. May I now be mindful of all of the teachers that surround me. I am grateful to them. I want to learn more throughout the rest of my life.

the present moment

I know I am breathing in. I know I am breathing out. I calm my body and mind. I smile. I dwell in the present moment. I know this is a wonderful moment.

A Note on Gathas

▲ ▼ ▲

Gatha is a Sanskrit term meaning "verse" or "hymn." In the *sutras* (Buddhist scripture), gathas can represent Buddhist teachings and praise of the virtues of Buddhas and bodhisattvas expressed in verse form. Some sutras are written entirely in verse, while others are written in prose interposed with sections of verse.

Chinese scholars have adopted this word for their versified compositions, which are known as *chieh* (abbreviation of *chieh-t'o*) or as *chieh-sang*, which is the combination of the Sanskrit and the Chinese. Some gathas go back centuries to the monastic practice of China and Vietnam.

In the Mahayana tradition, which encourages mindfulness in daily life as well as in meditation practice, gathas are short poems used in familiar situations each day, to remind us of how we can open to the moment and transform our lives.

The gathas I have written for this book are informal, but many contemporary gathas still retain the formal structure established in the "Purifying Practice" chapter of the Avatamsaka Sutra, a Mahayana scripture written several hundred years after the death of the Buddha. Robert Aitken, a Zen teacher, writes about the form: "The first line establishes the occasion, the second line presents the act of vowing, and the last two lines follow through with the specific conduct that one promises to undertake in these circumstances."

Thich Nhat Hanh has written a book called *Present Moment, Wonderful Moment,* which is a collection of mindfulness verses for daily living. He includes gathas about many things you do each and every day in a rather automatic manner. I highly recommend incorporating some of his gathas into your life as a way of reinforcing mindfulness practice. Please also consider composing some gathas of your own.

Index of Gathas

About the Author

▲ ▼ ▲

Dr. Barbara Ann Kipfer is the author of more than 30 books, including the bestselling *14,000 Things to Be Happy About* (Workman Publishing) and Page-a-Day calendars based on it. She has also authored *Instant Karma*, *8,789 Words of Wisdom*, *The Wish List*, and *1,400 Things for Kids to Be Happy About*. Barbara holds a Ph.D. and M.Phil. in linguistics, a Ph.D. in archaeology, an M.A. in Buddhist studies, and a B.S. in physical education. She is Managing Editor/Chief Lexicographer for Dictionary.com and Thesaurus.com (Lexico). She has worked for such companies as Answers.com, Ask Jeeves, CNET, General Electric Research, Grolier, IBM Research, and Knowledge Adventure. Her lexicographic website is www.reference-wordsmith.com. She is a Registered Professional Archaeologist and has also taught meditation.